For the Teacher

This reproducible study guide consists of lessons to use in conjunction with a specific novel. Used together, the books and the guide provide an exciting supplement to the basal reader in your classroom. Written in chapter-by-chapter format, the guide contains a synopsis, pre-reading activities, vocabulary and comprehension exercises, as well as extension activities to be used as follow-up to the novel.

In a homogeneous classroom, whole class instruction with one title is appropriate. In a heterogeneous classroom, reading groups should be formed: each group works on a different novel on its reading level. Depending upon the length of time devoted to reading in the classroom, each novel, with its guide and accompanying lessons, may be completed in three to six weeks.

The benefits of using NOVEL-TIES are numerous. Students read good literature in the original, rather than in abridged or edited form. The good reading habits, formed by practice in focusing on interpretive comprehension and literary techniques, will be transferred to the books students read independently. Passive readers become active, avid readers.

Use of NOVEL-TIES for reading development should begin with distribution of the novel and a folder to each child. After students have had a chance to look through the book, the pre-reading activity should be distributed. Each page of the study guide can be duplicated and students can answer directly on these sheets or on additional paper. All work should be kept in the students' folders until the novel is completed.

SYNOPSIS

Alan and Naomi is the story of a young Jewish boy and girl who live in the same apartment building in the Bronx during World War II. When Alan first notices Naomi crouching near his apartment door tearing paper into little scraps, he assumes she is crazy. Although Alan is aware of the war in Europe and the anti-semitism in his own neighborhood, he is more interested in school activities and playing stickball with his friend Shaun. But on this particular day, Alan's mother makes a connection between the War and Naomi's behavior, changing Alan's perspective on life forever.

She tells Alan about the tragedy Naomi has endured: she was a witness to her father's death at the hands of the Nazis. Having recently come to America from Nazi-controlled France, she and her mother are now living with the Liebmans upstairs from Alan and his family. Alan's mother asks him to befriend Naomi to help heal the trauma she has suffered.

Alan reluctantly agrees to visit Naomi, who remains mute in his presence. Alan uses his Charlie McCarthy dummy to foster communication with Naomi in a non-threatening manner. Naomi in turn uses her doll Yvette as a medium of communication with Alan. Slowly and painstakingly, a bond develops between the two children so that they no longer need Charlie and Yvette as intermediaries.

Once Alan gains Naomi's trust, he comes to appreciate her intelligence and humor: their visits together become a source of great enjoyment. Naomi finally confides in Alan, telling him about the horror of her father's death and her own futile attempt to destroy his Resistance maps. As Alan spends more and more time with Naomi, he becomes less available to Shaun, who feels slighted and is curious about the cause of his friend's absence. Shaun's curiosity turns to anger as Alan keeps his relationship with Naomi a secret. It is not until Naomi takes her first tentative steps into the outside world and Shaun

sees Naomi and Alan together, that he solves the mystery that has eluded him until now. Because of his resentment, Shaun refuses to hear Alan's explanation and apology. Instead, he excludes his former best friend from his life, making Alan lonesome for male companionship.

Alan and Naomi become closer friends and Naomi is even able to attend school. She is a gifted student and is becoming comfortable in her new environment. Her progress ends abruptly one day when Joe Condello directs anti-semitic remarks at Alan and Naomi on their way home from school. Alan reacts violently to Joe's taunts by fighting with him in what turns out to be a bloody street battle. This sight recalls to Naomi the time of her father's death, causing her to retreat to a psychotic state worse than the one in which Alan had first found her. Naomi must be hospitalized, for her psychological wounds are too deep and her memories too strong to be swept aside, even by Alan's friendship and trust. The book ends on an uncertain note as each reader must decide whether Naomi will ever be well again.

PRE-READING ACTIVITIES

1. Naomi and her mother fled France during World War II. Research Hitler's rise to power in Germany and his strategy to exterminate the Jews throughout Europe. This genocide is now called the Holocaust.

2. Germany occupied three-fifths of France during World War II and established a government at Vichy that was allied to the German cause. Not all the French, however, accepted the Vichy government. The Frenchmen who attempted to resist the German onslaught and organized secret societies were known as the free French or the Resistance. The Germans, of course, did everything they could to destroy this movement. Who led the Resistance movement? What were some of its activities?

3. America at the time of World War II (1941-1945) was a place vastly different from the America of today. Find out about the styles, fads, and entertainment of the 1940's. You may have relatives who remember this time. Try to interview someone who lived through this period of history and share these memories with the class.

4. One of the most popular forms of entertainment during the 1940's was the radio program hosted by the ventriloquist, Edgar Bergen, and his doll Charlie McCarthy. If possible, find pictures of the two. Find out what other shows were popular at this time and compile a list of movie stars and entertainers who were well-known during World War II.

5. Namoi has a serious psychotic disorder. Find out about mental illness and the methods of treatment used. What facilities are available for treatment in your community?

THINK IT OVER

Below are statements that you may or may not believe to be true. If you agree with a statement, write *YES* next to it in the *YOU* column. If you disagree, write *NO*. After reading *Alan and Naomi*, reread each statement and tell how the author feels, writing *YES* if you feel he would agree, or *NO* if you feel he would disagree.

	YOU	*AUTHOR*
1. Young children usually recover from a traumatic event more easily than adults.		
2. Children find it easier than adults to accept someone who appears to be different.		
3. Everyone is affected when a country goes to war.		
4. A good deed is always rewarded in some way.		
5. There are some things that are difficult to discuss even with a good friend.		
6. Friendship between a boy and girl is rare.		
7. After spending time with another person, it is easier to understand that person's feelings.		

BACKGROUND INFORMATION

The French Resistance

In June of 1940, Hitler's dream of German domination of Europe came a step closer to reality when Germany occupied almost two-thirds of France. The French then formed a government at Vichy, under Marshall Petain, who openly co-operated with the German conquerors. While the Nazi war machine seemed to roll on with little opposition, the beginnings of resistance to Germany's occupation began. Individual acts of sabotage occurred: telephone wires were secretly cut so that communication among the Germans was hampered, railroad workers helped derail supplies, posters glorifying Germany were marked with Jewish stars, defying Hitler's virulent anti-semitism.

Slowly, individual acts of protest became organized into underground resistance groups aimed at thwarting Germany's war effort. The organizations, with names such as The Crusade, the Alliance, and Noah's Ark, created a secret network of Frenchmen who plotted against their German conquerors. They worked alongside British and American intelligence agencies, giving them vital information about the enemy. For example, one Resistance worker, known as "the Shrimp," repaired German lifeboat jackets and knew when submarine maneuvers were being planned.

These Frenchmen lived under constant danger because their activities, if revealed, would inevitably lead to their capture and death. Such horrifying retribution as Myron Levoy describes in *Alan and Naomi* kept Resistance members in fear, but sabotaging Hitler was more important. More terrifying than German punishment to these Frenchmen was the thought of Nazi dominance of their beloved homeland.

The Yiddish Language

Yiddish was once the primary language of Jewish people in Eastern Europe. While its main source is German, the Yiddish language adopted much of the vocabulary of the lands in which Jews lived. The language is written in Hebrew letters. Today, Yiddish is often the second language of Jews throughout the world. Even if the younger generation is not fluent in the language, certain words and phrases are well understood.

In this book the author uses several Yiddish phrases to give authenticity and local color to the family's dialogue. Here are some of the phrases used and their meanings:

meshuggenerr – crazy

mensh – man, person

tummel – noise

chozzerai – junk

Oy, Gott! – Oh, God! (an exclamation)

kvetching – complaining

CHAPTERS 1 and 2

Vocabulary: Words with similar meanings are synonyms. Replace each underlined word in the sentences below with its synonym from the Word Box.

WORD BOX		
contempt	demon	imaginary
sullen	moist	scarcely

1. The ground was <u>damp</u> after the evening shower.
2 The <u>grumpy</u> girl refused to smile at the boy's jokes.
3. After his accident, he was <u>hardly</u> able to walk.
4. He walked away, bouncing the ball with total <u>scorn</u>.
5. The characters in the book were <u>unreal</u>.
6. The screech of the door on its hinges made it sound like an angry cat or a long-tailed <u>devil</u>.

Questions:

1. How did Shaun show that he is Alan's good friend?
2. How did Naomi behave when Alan first saw her?
3. Why did Naomi remind Alan of a puppy?
4. What did Alan's mother tell him about Naomi's past?
5. What did Alan's parents ask him to do? Do you think their request was fair? What would you have done in his place?

Literary Device: Similes

Similes are comparisons between two seemingly unlike objects using the words "as" or "like." For example:

> The girl [Naomi] kept staring at the bat as if it were a python poised to strike.

What is being compared?

Why does Naomi react to the bat in this way?

Chapters 1 and 2 (cont.)

Writing Activity:

Alan's father tells him, "In our life, Alan, sometimes when we're young, sometimes when we're old, in our life, once or twice, we're called upon to do something we can't do, that we don't want to do, that we won't do. But we do it."

Write about a time you were asked to do something you didn't want to do. Tell whether or not you did the act and what happened as a result of your decision.

Literary Technique: Prediction

Readers often predict, or figure out in advance, what will happen in a story. Do you think Alan will agree to his parents' request? Why or why not?

CHAPTERS 3 and 4

Antonyms: Antonyms are words with opposite meanings. Draw a line from the word on the left to its antonym on the right. Then use each word on the left to complete the sentence below.

1. abruptly	a. stare
2. victim	b. rough
3. glance	c. criminal
4. relieved	d. slowly
5. sleek	e. irritated

. . . .

1. The cat's fur was ____________________ and glossy.
2. When my old boyfriend entered the room, I left the party ____________________.
3. Alan wondered if Naomi herself had been a ____________________ of the Nazis.
4. After studying for days, I was ____________________ when the test was over.
5. I didn't want the teacher to see me ____________________ at the clock, hoping class would soon end.

Questions:

1. What was Alan hoping Naomi's torn map would reveal about Naomi and her mother? Why did he feel this way?
2. How did Alan get Naomi to respond to him?
3. Why did Alan decide to help Naomi?
4. How did Alan's parents react when he agreed to help Naomi?
5. Why did Alan decide to keep his relationship with Naomi a secret from Shaun?

Decision-Making:

Before Alan came to his decision, he weighed the reasons for helping Naomi against the reasons for rejecting his parents request. Put yourself into Alan's place as he tried to work through his problem by writing all the reasons he should or should not help Naomi.

CHAPTERS 5, 6 and 7

Vocabulary: Words can be used in more than one way. Knowing the meaning of a word can help you figure out how it is being used in a new context. Use each of the definitions below to answer the following questions.

1. If a blank is unmarked, what is a blank expression?

   ____

2. If water that gushes flows out in full force, when would somebody's speech be described as gushing?

   ____

3. If a dash is a short, fast race, what does it mean to dash off a note?

   ____

4. If an alarm is a signal that warns of danger, what does a look of alarm on someone's face tell you?

   ____

5. If a cup is a small container shaped like a bowl, when might you cup your hands?

   ____

Questions:

1. How did Naomi communicate with Alan? Why do you think this was the only way she would communicate?
2. Alan had once helped his mother in the same way that he was now trying to help Naomi. What had he done? Why do you think this method could be successful?
3. How did Mrs. Landley react to Alan's and Shaun's butterfly joke? What does this tell you about Mrs. Landley's character?
4. Why was Alan annoyed with Shaun?
5. How did Naomi show Alan that she wanted him to visit again?

Writing Activity:

At this point in the story, Naomi's feelings about Alan are changing. Imagine that you are Naomi and are willing to write your thoughts about Alan in a journal. Write a journal entry describing the things you have done with Alan and your changing feelings toward him.

CHAPTERS 8, 9 and 10

Vocabulary: Reading a word in context can sometimes help you figure out its meaning. Read each sentence below and tell what you think the underlined word means. Compare your definitions to those in the dictionary.

1. There's no planes around. Just Spitfires camouflaged to look like sea gulls.
   Your definition: ______________________________
   Dictionary: ______________________________

2. That evening, Alan sensed that Naomi was better the moment he walked into her room.
   Your definition: ______________________________
   Dictionary: ______________________________

3. With her hand over her mouth, in a faint voice, Naomi said for the doll, "Uh...uhkay."
   Your definition: ______________________________
   Dictionary: ______________________________

4. Alan was just learning "La Marseilles," the French national anthem, in school.
   Your definition: ______________________________
   Dictionary: ______________________________

5. As if he needed protection. As if he were some sort of delicate flower.
   Your definition: ______________________________
   Dictionary: ______________________________

Questions:

1. Why did Alan decide one day to play stickball instead of visiting Naomi?
2. Why did Alan's father insist that Alan see Naomi after dinner even though he had homework to do? Do you think he was right?
3. Why did Naomi get upset when "Charlie" called her Naomi instead of Yvette?
4. What made Alan continue to keep Naomi a secret from Shaun?
5. Why do you think Naomi was upset when "Charlie" sang "La Marseilles"?
6. Name some of the things that show Naomi is slowly improving.

Chapters 8, 9 and 10 (cont.)

Question for further discussion:

In many ways Alan is a dutiful son, helping Naomi even at times when he felt it was hopeless and unfair. Do you think you would be as obedient? Explain. If you can, tell about a time when you agreed to your parents' wishes even though you didn't want to.

Literary Devices:

1. **Simile** – a comparison between two unlike objects using the words "like" or "as."

   What is being compared in this simile:

   > But she [Naomi] was as hard to catch and hold as a shiny droplet of mercury.

   What does this tell you about Naomi?

2. **Metaphor** – an implied comparison between two unlike objects.

   What is being compared in this metaphor:

   > Alan felt those snakes in his stomach twisting again.

   How does Alan feel and why does he feel this way?

3. **Personification** – a literay device in which an author gives life-like qualities to inanimate objects. For example:

   > The umbrellas seemed to be in mourning again.

   What human characteristic are umbrellas given in this sentence?

CHAPTERS 11, 12, 13 and 14

Vocabulary: Some words in our language have more than one meaning. They have to be read in context to determine which meaning is appropriate. Read the following pairs of sentences and decide which meaning fits the underlined word.

1. The team had an incredible winning streak, beating every team they faced during the season. ________
2. The dog had a mean streak, making him a better guard dog than pet. ________
   a. trait or temperament
   b. a period, a length of time.

3. On a diet it is necessary to curb your appetite. ________
4. Step onto the curb when you get out of the taxi. ________
   a. to restrain or control
   b. a concrete or stone edging of a sidewalk

5. I read the newspaper every day so I can be knowledgeable about current events. ________
6. I was afraid to swim in the ocean because of the strong current. ________
   a. a flow of water or air
   b. of the present time, now going on

7. A static mind will not produce exciting new ideas. ________
8. His voice was unclear because of the static on the radio. ________
   a. crackling sounds interrupting a transmission
   b. not active, unchanging

Questions:

1. What was different about Naomi when Alan saw her after his trip to the library? What did they do together during this visit?
2. Describe how Alan acted when he saw Naomi in the lobby. Why did he behave this way?

Chapters 11, 12, 13 and 14 (cont.)

3. Why did Naomi's doctor want her to give up Yvette? Why was this so difficult for Naomi?
4. How did Naomi behave when Alan spoke to her directly and called her by her name?
5. Describe Alan's feelings when he leaves Naomi. Do you think he is being fair to himself?

Activity:

Do you see any change in Alan's feelings towards Naomi? Find some examples from the book that show the development of Naomi and Alan's friendship. Be prepared to share them with the class.

CHAPTERS 15, 16, 17 and 18

Vocabulary: Word analogies are equations in which the first pair of words have the same relationship as the second pair of words. For example: DAY is to NIGHT as FUTURE is to PAST. Both pairs of words are opposites. Complete each of the analogies below with a word from the Word Box.

WORD BOX	
reluctant	opulence
insight	vicious
sulk	

1. GENTLE is to ___________________ as DOUBT is to TRUST.

2. EAGER is to WILLING as ___________________ is to HESITANT.

3. TENSE is to NERVOUS as UNDERSTANDING is to ___________________.

4. LUXURY is to ___________________ as CONFUSION is to BEWILDERMENT.

5. ___________________ is to SADNESS as GRIN is to HAPPINESS.

Questions:

1. Why did the Liebmans and Mrs. Kirshenbaum decide to give Alan a "day off"?
2. What made Alan realize that Naomi had to give up Yvette?
3. What was it that Alan and his mother decided was a victory? How had this happened?
4. What was the importance of Naomi saying Alan's name?

Question for further discussion:

During World War II, people were continually reminded that we were at war with Germany. Although there was no actual fighting on American soil, the war was brought home in other ways. How did the author show that America was very much involved in war?

Chapters 15, 16, 17 and 18 (cont.)

Writing Activity:

While Alan was at the movies on his "day off" from Naomi, he thought that it was "good to not have to be Alan Silverman for a while. To not have to be anyone at all." Write about a time when you felt you needed to escape from a problem. Tell what you did and how you felt afterwards.

CHAPTERS 19, 20, 21 and 22

Vocabulary: There are many words in our language that appear in different forms as different parts of speech.

For example:

repetition - noun

repeat - verb

repetitive - adjective

Fill in the blanks in the word chart below providing other forms of the given words. Then choose one word from the word list to complete the following sentences.

NOUN a person, place, or thing	VERB an action word	ADJECTIVE a describing word
1.		admirable
2. abandonment		
3.	astonish	
4.		aggravating

1. Volunteering at the hospital was an _______________ thing to do.

2. You can imagine his _______________ when he won the lottery.

3. You will _______________ the injury if you refuse to rest.

4. We found the _______________ cat meowing on our front steps.

Chapters 19, 20, 21 and 22 (cont.)

Questions:

1. What surprises did Alan meet when Mrs. Landley called him in for a conference?
2. Why do you think Alan was able to reassure Naomi during the air raid whereas the grown-ups could not?
3. Why was Alan pleased with himself even though he had struck out in the baseball game?
4. What new behavior did Naomi show on the day she and Alan went out alone?

Writing Activity:

Alan's day with Naomi at the abandoned airport was special in many ways. Write about a special time you have had with a good friend and what made this day important to you.

CHAPTERS 23, 24, 25 and 26

Vocabulary: Use the context to select the best meaning for each underlined word from the choices below the sentence.

1. He hesitated meeting Naomi because she seemed so strange and melancholy.

   a. joyous b. sad c. sick

2. They walked together in glum silence, neither one willing to smile.

   a. cheerful b. gloomy c. quiet

3. "Hey, what do you want?" bellowed Alan in his loudest voice.

   a. laughed b. whispered c. shouted

4. He studied the ceiling and knew every blemish, every spot where the paint was peeling.

   a. imperfection b. ornament c. improvement

5. She nodded her head in silent assent.

   a. denial b. agreement c. explanation

Questions:

1. Why did Naomi blame herself for her father's death?
2. What made Alan get angry at Shaun?
3. Why had Shaun been angry at Alan? Why did this make Alan feel stupid?
4. Why did Alan resent it when Mrs. Liebman thanked him for helping Naomi?

Prediction:

What do you think Naomi's first day at school will be like? What things might be difficult for her? How might Alan help her?

CHAPTERS 27, 28, 29, 30

Vocabulary: Our language has words to express different degrees of a single idea. For example, *throw* means to send through the air with a motion of your arm; while *hurl* means to throw with great force. Draw a line from each word on the left to the word on the right that expresses a greater degree of the same idea.

1. smile	a. laugh
2. dislike	b. stare
3. squeeze	c. detest
4. titter	d. crush
5. look	e. beam

Questions:

1. How did Mrs. Landley help Naomi relax on her first day of school?
2. When Alan and Naomi are asked to write about a friend or relative, whom do they choose? What do their choices reveal about their relationship?
3. Why do you think Joe Condello picked a fight with Alan? Why did Alan become so enraged this time?
4. What caused Shaun and Alan to resume their friendship?
5. What did Alan mean when he said, "Naomi's gone. She completely disappeared. Like a light goes out in a room"?
6. Why do you think the street fight had such a terrible effect on Naomi?
7. At the end of the book, how do you know that Naomi is in a poorer mental state than she was when Alan met her?

Writing Activity:

Choose one of the following:

1. Write a different ending to this story.
2. Write a letter to the author telling him how you feel about the book. Include your opinion about the ending.

CLOZE ACTIVITY

The following passage has been taken from Chapter 16. Read it through and then fill in each blank with a word that makes sense. Then, you can compare your language with that of the author.

Alan made way for Naomi. She walked past him, head down, ____________[1] the living room. Then she looked ____________[2] slowly, and stared at herself in ____________[3] large mirror on the wall. Alan ____________[4] know what to say, so he ____________[5] walked over to Naomi and stood ____________[6] to her, looking in the mirror. ____________[7] he raised his hand and waved.

"Hello," ____________[8] Alan, but his voice sounded hollow ____________[9] him.

Naomi continued to stare at ____________[10] mirror. Her fear made the room ____________[11] them seem cold and unfriendly, like ____________[12] waiting room in the doctor's office.

"____________[13] that?" asked Alan, pointing at his reflection in the mirror. There was a ____________[14] silence. Then Alan decided to answer ____________[15] own question. "That's me. Alan Silverman. ____________[16] known as A. A. Bloomladle."

"Charlie?" said Naomi very ____________.[17]

"Charlie's in the hospital getting fixed up."

Naomi sat down abruptly on the carpet and started tearing the paper in her hand.

POST-READING

1. Look back at the "Think It Over" activity at the beginning of the study guide. Now tell what you believe the author would feel about each statement. If you think he would agree, write "yes." If you feel he would disagree, write "no."

2. What do you think the future holds for Naomi? Do you think Naomi will ever recover, or are her psychological wounds too deep? Write a short paragraph telling why you feel the way you do.

3. Sometimes an event has such a profound influence on us that it affects us for the rest of our lives. How do you feel Alan's experiences with Naomi will change him? What kind of adult do you think Alan will become? Speculate on what you think Alan might be like as he matures. It would be interesting to share these predictions with the other students and see if theirs are similar.

4. Although the ending of *Alan and Naomi* is not a reassuring one, there are many real-life "Naomis" who experienced the horror of the Holocaust first hand and were able to build new and satisfying lives despite the scars left by their tormentors. Invite a Holocaust survivor to the classroom to talk about personal experiences and survival afterwards.

5. Besides being a story that deals with the Holocaust, *Alan and Naomi* is also the story of a special friendship. Do you have a friendship in your own life that is as important as the one between Alan and Naomi, or do you think deep friendships require a shared tragedy? Explain your opinion.

6. Do you think Alan's parents had the right to ask Alan to sacrifice so much of his life for Naomi's sake?

7. It has been said that the real tragedy of war can only be understood when we see it through the eyes of a single person. Did this book help you to understand the tragedy of the Holocaust and the horrors inflicted by Hitler, or do you think your understanding would have been better if the book dealt with the experiences of many Jewish families in Europe during the war? Explain your answer.

ANSWER KEY

Chapters 1, 2 -

Vocabulary: 1. moist 2. sullen 3. scarcely 4. contempt 5. imaginary 6. demon

Questions: 1. He protected Alan from Joe Condello and prevented Alan from getting hurt. 2. She was kneeling near his door tearing paper into scraps. 3. Her eyes had the same sad and frightened look. 4. She and her mother had escaped from the Nazis; Naomi had seen her father beaten to death when it was discovered he had joined the French Resistance. 5. They wanted him to play with Naomi, spending an hour with her every day. Answers will vary to the last parts of the question.

Chapters 3, 4 -

Vocabulary: 1. d 2. c 3. a 4. e 5. b; 1. sleek 2. abruptly 3. victim 4. relieved 5. glance

Questions: 1. Alan was hoping the map would reveal that Naomi and her mother were really Nazi spies. Then he would not have to feel guilty if he did not help Naomi. 2. He used his Charlie McCarthy dummy as a means to get her to talk. 3. He realized that Naomi needed him. 4. His parents had tears in their eyes because they were thrilled with Alan's decision. 5. Shaun started to tease Alan, saying he was a sissy.

Chapters 5, 6, 7 -

Vocabulary: 1. a face that shows no emotion 2. when words flow ceaselessly without containing any meaning 3. to write a note very quickly 4. that the person is terrified 5. when you need to drink from your hands as at a stream

Questions: 1. She used her doll Yvette. Answers will vary to the second part of the question. 2. Alan's mother had lost a newborn child, and his mother sat alone in her bedroom. Alan started to talk to her as if she were listening. 3. Mrs. Landley told the class that this was a wonderful way to celebrate a poem. Answers will vary to the second part of the question. 4. Shaun did not release his moths; instead, he sat and laughed. 5. The doll Yvette asked Charlie to visit again.

Chapters 8, 9,10 -

Vocabulary: 1. camouflaged - disguised, hidden 2. sensed - became aware of 3. faint - weak, not strong 4. anthem - official song of a country 5. delicate - fragile, sensitive

Questions: 1. He wanted to be with his friends and the weather had cleared after the rain. 2. He felt it was more important for his son to help Naomi than it was for him to do anything else. Answers will vary to the second part of the question. 3. She wasn't ready to speak directly to Alan. Yvette still had to do the talking. 4. Shaun made fun of Naomi, calling her "Crazy Cat." 5. Answers will vary, but should include the idea that any allusions to France remind her of the atrocities she has experienced. 6. Even though she still speaks through Yvette's voice, she asks for Charlie to return, engages in conversation, laughs, and admits that she needs a friend.

Chapters 11, 12, 13, 14 -

Vocabulary: 1. b 2. a 3. a 4. b 5. b 6. a 7. b 8. a

Questions: 1. Naomi seemed relaxed and there were no paper scraps anywhere. They sang together. 2. Alan wanted Naomi to leave him alone and he tried to ignore her. Naomi is still too frightened to communicate without the dummy as intermediary. 3. The doctor wanted Naomi to become part of the real world. Naomi was using the doll as a way to protect herself from participating in the world around her. 4. She screamed, "Non!" grabbing the Charlie McCarthy doll and throwing it against the wall. Then she hid under the bed. 5. He felt stupid because he blamed himself for bringing on Naomi's uncontrolled behavior. Answers will vary to the second part of the question.

Chapters 15, 16, 17, 18 -

Vocabulary: 1. vicious 2. reluctant 3. insight 4. opulence 5. sulk

Questions: 1. Everyone felt bad that Alan feared he had caused Naomi's outburst. 2. He watched the girls at the movies and knew Naomi ultimately had to become more like them if she was going to be well. 3. It was a victory when Naomi spoke without using Yvette as an intermediary. Naomi had been sent to visit at Alan's house without her doll, and Alan did not make his dummy available. Alan moved slowly and painstakingly, initially talking to a mirror reflection of Naomi. 4. It shows that she is taking an important step toward independence and emotional well-being. She does not need to depend on the dolls in order to trust and communicate with another person.

Chapters 19, 20, 21, 22 -

Vocabulary: 1. admiration, admire, admirable 2. abandonment, abandon, abandoned 3. astonishment, astonish, astonishing 4. aggravation, aggravate, aggravating; 1. admirable 2. astonishment 3. aggravate 4. abandoned

Questions: 1. She knew he was helping Naomi; she knew all about Naomi and explained that she was an extemely bright girl who would benefit from Alan's tutoring in schoolwork; and that she thought he was a great kid. 2. Answers will vary, but should include the idea that Alan could address the situation at her emotional level and inject the scene with humor. 3. Naomi had not revealed their friendship when she passed by, and Alan had successfully put down the other boys for calling Naomi names. 4. She ran and played in a carefree, childlike manner. It made her seem almost normal.

Chapters 23, 24, 25, 26 -

Vocabulary: 1. b 2. b 3. c 4. a 5. b

Questions: 1. She didn't destroy the maps fast enough. She thought this had caused her father's death at the hands of the Gestapo. Alan was deeply moved and assured Naomi that he would be there for her whenever she needed him - even at a time when his male friends were around. 2. Shaun saw Naomi with Alan and called Alan "a sissy." 3. Shaun was hurt that Alan did not tell him about his secret friendship with Naomi. Alan felt stupid because he hadn't trusted his friend to understand about Naomi. 4. Alan was Naomi's friend, and he was helping her out of friendship. It was not to please anyone else.

Chapters 27, 28, 29, 30 -

Vocabulary: 1. e 2. c 3. d 4. a 5. b

Questions: 1. She welcomed Naomi, she spoke softly to her, and she included Naomi in class discussion. 2. They choose one another; this shows the strength of the bond between them. 3. Answers will vary to this question, but could include the ideas that Joe is anti-semitic and/or jealous of

Alan for having Naomi as a girlfriend. 4. Shaun took up Alan's cause in his street fight with Joe Condello. After that, their friendship resumes automatically. 5. The personality of the girl that he had come to know and love has been replaced by a psychotic Naomi, unrecognizable to him. 6. The street fight reminded Naomi of the Nazis killing her father. She was not yet strong enough emotionally to separate the two incidents. 7. She refuses to talk – not even to Charlie McCarthy.